A Life

© 2018 Nancy Tomich • All rights reserved
Dayton Publishing LLC • Solana Beach, California
ISBN-13: 978-1-7325265-1-8

A Life
Ethel Frieda Bender

My mother, Ethel Frieda Bender, wrote most of the story on the pages in this book. She had planned to do an entire memoir but was unable to complete it. As her daughter, I have added opening and closing sections and done a wee bit of editing. Ethel was a strong woman who led a hard but happy life. She loved reading and writing. Putting her words into a book would have pleased her enormously. This really is for you, Mom.

— Nancy Tomich

My name is Ethel Frieda Bender. I am 91 years old as I write this, the pull of childhood memories growing stronger as each day passes. I soak myself in them, knowing that the time to relive them is waning. The future holds no promise; the present offers only the pains of old age. Ah, but the past, that is where comfort lies — the story I have written in space and time. My recollections are fragmented and probably not always accurate. I present them here not as a timeline but rather as snippets that have remained with me across decades.

Ten Years on a Farm

Raw and unbelievably cold weather marked winter in 1910 in the central Illinois countryside. The tall, lean, young farmhand slept and ate in an unheated cabin on the farm where he worked. At age 23, he had a sharp mind and two willing hands. In the early 1900's education for farm boys was meager, but he had managed to attend a little one-room school until fourth grade. After that, his days were spent plowing, planting, weeding, and tending crops and livestock.

In February, 1911, Nicholas Christian Bender had a horrendous cold and was miserable in his little log cabin. I try to imagine how he felt — alone, trying to work but unable, and knowing that one of the most important times in his life lay just ahead. He and Magdalena Marie Blinn were to be married in Belleville on Valentine's Day. Reverend Pessel had been sent a letter asking him to perform the ceremony.

When the day arrived for the drive to the church, Nicholas was too ill with double pneumonia to go. There were no telephones, and no additional letter was sent to the minister. So Reverend Pessel thought there had been a quarrel or misunderstanding — in a way, he was left standing at the altar. Desperate, young Nicholas finally went to his parents' home for help, where his sweetheart finally found

The family farm where Nicholas Bender lived as a child

him and nursed him through his illness. His father had given up on him, figuring he was going to die, but Magdalena was tenacious. Finally, on May 9, 1911, Nicholas Bender and Magdalena Blinn, attended by his brother Louis and her sister Annie, were married — and Reverend Pessel now knew what had happened.

The young couple farmed near Freeburg, Illinois, and a son, Frederick Christian Bender (Freddie), was born on May 24, 1912. Grandpa Bender (Nicholas' father) — who had declined to help Nicholas when he was severely ill with pneumonia — wanted to claim some livestock on the young couple's farm for his own. Consequently, they moved away to Shiloh Valley, where they rented a farm near a proposed airfield (now Scott Air Force Base). There they farmed 300 acres, with few comforts or modern machinery.

In 1915, I (Ethel Frieda Bender) was born on March 28. Freddie was my adoring (and adored) older brother. We spent a happy childhood in the large shady yard surrounding the farmhouse, often wading in a nearby creek. There were also plenty of cats and kittens to play with. Times were hard, and Nicholas

Nicholas Christian Bender and Magdalena Marie Blinn (seated) were married on May 9, 1911, attended by her sister Annie Blinn and his brother Louis Bender.

and Magdalena grew most of the garden produce they needed. They traded butter, eggs, and vegetables for flour, sugar, and other staples. The washing machine was hand-powered until a small gasoline engine was attached later — a true luxury. Dad taught himself to do such things, saying "You don't need a teacher to tell you how to do something — you can learn it yourself if you want to." And he did learn to design and build most anything.

In 1917, we had our first Model T Ford, and later on acquired a Fordson tractor. We had horses: Queenie, Bess, Puss, and Jack. They were workhorses only and were always well-fed and cared for. Dad put in a water trough fed by a pipe from the well so they always had fresh water.

I was very small (perhaps four or five) when Dad's younger brother, Uncle George, came to stay with us. Grandpa Bender had succeeded in alienating another of his sons. (In addition to Nicholas and George, Uncle Ed was a brother who was alienated — he joined the army and left for Texas.) My greatest memory of Uncle George was of his sitting on the well-house steps (we did have very good well water).

He would whittle little whistles from willow twigs for us. And when he made Freddie a corncob pipe, I cried until he made me one, too. I always had to have whatever Freddie had. Uncle George stayed quite a while and then left, and we never heard from him again.

People, mostly relatives, came to stay every once in a while. I, of course, especially recall Uncle George, and I remember a cousin of Mom's, old Pete, who helped with the farm work in exchange for a place in the barn to sleep and for food.

The house on the farm originally had just three rooms. Another room, called the "new room," was added later. A lean-to stood at the back door — sort of an enclosed porch that we called a shed. The property was a rural botanic garden, with apple, peach, and pear trees, grape arbors, and plants.

Mom's cousin from Carlyle, Louisa German, came to stay with us a few weeks. She, of course, had the new bedroom. She was of some help to Mom, but did not exert herself. Freddie and I decided that "she cramped our style" and that maybe we could encourage her to leave. Freddie caught a huge grasshopper, marched up to Cousin Louisa, as we were told to address her, and put it down her back. What an uproar! She was scared to death of it. I can't recall being punished when Cousin Louisa left, saying that "she wouldn't stay with children like us." I don't think that Mom and Dad were unhappy about her leaving at all. I have not had the nerve to catch a bug since, though, and still will not touch grasshoppers, worms, and doodlebugs. I can recall that, later in Belleville, Mom dug up our garden one spring day and forked over some dirt containing some worms. She picked up one and threw it at me in fun. I was horrified when it went down my blouse. Mom just laughed at me. "They don't bite," she said. To this day, I still hate worms.

Freddie and I were allowed to play all around the barn and in the fields and to wade in the creek. We loved to slide down the stacks of wheat straw after harvest. There were no combines then, only binders that tied the wheat or oats into bundles. These bundles were piled into shocks. Two of the bundles were stood together and six to eight others were grouped around them. The shocks remained this way until the threshing crew (all of the neighbors worked together

Frederick Christian Bender (Freddie) and Ethel Frieda Bender c. 1920

to help each other in this chore) processed them. One neighbor had a steam engine that powered the thresher separator. This would separate the seeds/grains of wheat from the straw. The grain was collected in cloth sacks, and the chaff or straw was blown into large stacks. The clean grain was then moved to the granary to be sold to a grain elevator or fed to the farm animals.

When harvest was over, in our field stood a huge stack of straw, perhaps fifteen feet tall and as big around as our house. It was great fun sliding down this stack, climbing up the stack, sliding down, and doing this over and over again. How full of chaff and straw we would get — all itchy and dirty. Once, Freddie saw a hole in the stack of straw that was round and neat. What could have made such a hole — maybe a fuzzy baby rabbit? Curiosity got the best of him and he reached into the hole to see. But a mama rabbit was there and it really bit his hand. We took off for home and got a good scolding for being so silly as to reach into a rabbit burrow.

I particularly loved the harvest (wheat and oats) — the threshing and the haymaking. These were both done in the summer, and that is when Dad needed help. In the winter months, there was the butchering that occurred around Thanksgiving. October through January was spent as "stay-inside" time, with husking and shelling corn ears, oiling the harness, and other inside chores.

Whenever we had extra hired help, Mom made special noontime dinners. When Mom could not cook enough or needed extra supplies, we drove to Belleville. In summer, this often meant getting a large bologna about two feet long and five to six inches around. We also got a five-pound brick of cheese and baker bread — a real treat. At harvest and threshing, Mom would bake two or three cakes plus several pies. Lunch was at 9 a.m., dinner at 12–1 p.m., lunch at 3 p.m., and supper, a light meal, at 7:30 or 8 p.m., whenever the men quit working. The leaves for our table (all twelve of them) were put in, and the large table filled our dining area. We had six chairs; these were not enough for the harvest workforce, so benches were brought in from our yard. The men washed up at the pump with cold water from the well and then ate their fill. Then, Freddie and I ate with the women and any children the neighbors had brought along.

I had never tasted coffee and watched one hired hand drink several cups with cream and sugar in it. I begged Mom to let me drink some like that. It tasted awful.

A neighbor up Shiloh Hill from our farm often came to visit Mom. She always brought peaches, made cookies, or, on my birthday, made me cream puffs. While Mom worked and talked, "Auntie Boettcher," as I called her, made a new dress for Susie, my doll. Susie was my only toy, and I loved her. I can remember falling out the back door and breaking her china head. I cried and cried until Dad came in and said, "You sing so pretty, sing some more!" He made me so angry that I stopped crying. The next trip to Belleville, Susie got a new head, but she just wasn't the same.

We were always going out to the big old barn to play. Out of the wind and weather, the barn was warm and pleasant. It smelled of sweet hay and grain, of leather harnesses, and of the oil needed to keep the leather soft and supple. We could go up to the hayloft by climbing a ladder that went through an open space in the floor of the loft. You had to watch which direction you took in sliding down the mounds of hay stacked in the loft: Many times, cats and kittens would be bedded down there. We played with the cats and kittens, too. They kept the barn free of mice and rats. Dad would feed them milk directly from the cows when he was milking. One day, Freddie and I grew tired of the hayloft, and, even though Dad told us to stay off the machinery on the bottom floor of the barn, we decided to play in the wagon part of the manure spreader. It consisted of sort of a wagon with a spinning, pronged wheel to distribute the manure or fertilizer.

Well, we just had to find out if we could make the pronged wheel spin. So Freddie gave it a good yank. Sure enough, it spun around. But I was too close and one of the prongs sliced open my right leg. I wasn't seven yet, and I really screamed. Mom calmly washed the cut, applied peroxide, and then bandaged my leg. Then she said "go and play and stay out of the barn!"

We had a creek some distance from the yard. Dad cut steps into the steep bank so we could walk down to ankle-deep water and sand to play. The creek was a fascinating place, and in hot weather the lovely cool water was soothing. One Sunday in spring, Aunt Frieda, Uncle Butch, and their family (Edwin, Leroy, and

Helen) came to visit. Sunday was a "no-work" day and the time to go visiting or to receive company. This particular Sunday was a nice day, but not warm enough to go barefoot or wading, or so we were told. We went down to the sandbar in the creek under some plum trees, where we could not be seen from the house. We took our shoes off — to wade just a little. We were having a great time when Lee, as we called Leroy, found a group of crawfish holes. (The crawfish made holes to sleep in the soft mud at the water's edge.) Lee stepped on a hole and the pincer of a big old crawfish closed on his toe and would not let go. Lee started yelling loudly, and, of course, our parents heard him and came running. As you can guess, we all got into trouble. I can't recall how we got the crawdad to let go — but it was exciting.

Our farm, which we rented from a wealthy Belleville family, was near the newly established Scott Air Force Base, or Scott Field as it was known then. (The farm later became part of Scott.) One day I went to Belleville in the Model T Ford with Dad. We drove out of our farm lane onto a dirt road and then turned onto a cinder road, where four soldiers stood thumbing a ride. Dad stopped to pick them up, and they climbed into the car, which became quite crowded. One soldier had to hold me on his lap. I was petrified. In fact, I can still feel just how terrified I was when I think about it.

The people we rented from had a large home about a mile to a mile and a half away. Our telephone was connected to a six-family party line. The phone itself was hand-cranked and mounted on the wall. You could "listen in" to other conversations on the party line. Each family had its own distinctive ring — one long, two longs, a long and a short, etc. I think ours was a long and two shorts. There were Bell and Kinloch telephones. We had a Bell phone. Grandma Blinn had a Kinloch, so it was a long-distance call to her house. One night a common emergency ring sounded: Our landlord's house had caught on fire. All the neighbors and the Scott Field fire department were there, but, with limited water and a large fire, the house was ultimately completely destroyed. Being that our landlord was wealthy, the family had an elegant bathtub (we used a tin tub). Dad helped neighbors carry furniture from the burning house. He was almost badly hurt or killed when stairs from the upstairs (where the bathroom was) broke under the weight of the heavy tub. It was close to Christmas, and we had wanted to put candles on our Christmas tree as we had done before. But after coming home from the fire, Dad said that candles were OUT!! The fire in our landlord's house had started either from candles or from sparks from the steam engine on the train that ran to Scott Field.

A nearby farm family, the Seibert's (Mr. and Mrs., Paula, Alvena, Ben, and Victor), took us to school. Initially, Alvena and Ben took Freddie, and when I started school, I got to go with them in their pony cart. It was over two miles to the Shiloh Village School. Miss Beason was my first grade and second grade teacher. We got water from a pump and the toilets were outside. One day as I was waiting for Freddie, who was in the sixth grade (they had an hour longer school day than the lower grades), I went outside to the toilets. A group of kids was playing baseball nearby, and, as I passed near them, the one who was batting hit the ball and got so excited that he slung the bat and hit me in the chest. I passed out and woke up on the teacher's desk. And I guess I was dizzy. The teacher and several other people who were there did not know what to do for me — so they did nothing. There were no paramedics, no ambulances and not even a doctor in Shiloh then. You did what you could if someone was injured. If you ended up okay — fine — and if you were not, there was not much anyone could do. I don't know if Mom and Dad ever knew about it. The teacher continued to care for me, and, by the time Freddie got out of class, I was feeling well enough to go home. We rode the pony cart. The pony was stabled at a shed near the school. We were so lucky — most kids had to walk to school.

The Shiloh school encompassed eight grades and had a good-sized play area. It had been rebuilt and was then a two-story building with four classrooms. On the lower floor, the first and second grades were in one classroom, and the third and fourth grades were in a second classroom. On the second floor, the fifth and sixth grades were in one classroom and the seventh and eighth grades were in a second classroom.

One day, for whatever reason, Vic Seibert and I walked home. The dirt roads were dusty and we must have been really dirty when we got home. At that time in the early 1920's, one could see raccoons, skunks, and an occasional fox. Rabbits were everywhere. Two boys that lived along the road from the school near our farm had encountered a skunk. Either they got in its way or their dog did, and the skunk sprayed them with "perfume." Those two boys did not show up for school for several days. After meeting the skunk, they had to undress outdoors and their clothes were burned. They took several baths a day for several days in soda water (now tomato juice is used).

Once, Mom's brother, Otto Blinn, brought his then girlfriend, Linda Brutto, to visit. It was past my bedtime and I did not want to leave the company. Linda said, "Be a good girl and go to bed; I'll bring you some candy the next time we come." She forgot this promise — but I never forgot. Otto and Linda were married at St. Peter's Cathedral on Thanksgiving Day in about 1923. Linda's family was fairly well-off. They owned a dairy farm on the Freeburg Road, and the reception was held at their home. Linda's brother Ollie had something no one had seen before — a radio! It was a crystal set. By putting on earphones and being very quiet, you could hear music as the dials were turned. We all had a turn listening to that amazing contraption (can you imagine how seeing TV and computers would shake up everyone from that era?).

I was eight years old at that time, and when a special delivery letter came for Aunt Linda, we all crowded around to see and hear. The letter told of friends of Aunt Linda who had come down with scarlet fever and could not attend her wedding and reception.

Scarlet fever was terrible back then, with no penicillin or other antibiotics. I may have been close enough to the letter to contact some bacteria on the paper. Or there may have been another cause, but two weeks after that Thanksgiving wedding I became sick. As I got sicker and sicker, it was diagnosed as scarlet fever. I spent three months in bed and missed four months of school. Our whole family — Mom, Dad, Freddie, Mildred (my younger sister), and me — all ill at the same time. I was delirious part of the time and saw Christmas things that were not there. I later found out that we had not had Christmas that year — no tree and no gifts. Freddie was told by the doctor that he was better and could get up and would be able to go to school in a week or so. But he died the night after the doctor's visit. I was devastated. I still find it hard to deal with.

In addition to everything else, a vein in Mom's throat burst. It was a terrible December. Neighbors had fed and cared for our horses and cattle, but no one was allowed to come close to our house. We did have a nurse that the doctor sent to help us. I hated her — she ate all the cookies that the Shiloh Valley Grange sent for us. Our house had to be fumigated to kill the germs. Health authorities came and pulled everything apart, sealed all doors and windows, and then burned some sort of gunk to fumigate the house. Mom and Dad were even unable to go to Freddie's funeral. As I look back at all this, Mom and Dad had to be very strong individuals to be able to bear it all. No wonder they did not want to stay on the farm, especially with no son growing up to help with the work. And in two years, we moved to Belleville.

I imagine it took two years of crops from the farm to be able to buy the house and four acres of land we had on Lebanon Avenue in Belleville. The house was a mess until Dad remodeled it. Before the scarlet fever I had two fat, blond braids that I hated. But Mom and Dad had been proud of my big braids. Then, because of the illness, my hair was either cut or came out with the high fever that I had. Afterwards, I had short hair. I had lost quite a bit of weight and was a mess by the time I went to school in Belleville. I went to Jefferson for fourth grade, Bunsen for fifth grade, and then back to Jefferson for sixth grade (they added a top floor and more classrooms to Jefferson, so I could go back there for sixth grade). I was told, while in the fifth grade, to get my eyes examined. Not many children even went for eye exams then. I had to get glasses, and, from that time, was teased and tormented. They called me four-eyes, goofy eyes, etc., and heckled me by yelling "think you're so smart for wearing cheaters." I was shy about taking my glasses off, but they soon became my best friend.

One of the girls at school was bossy and a smart aleck. If she told you that you could not play at recess, you could not play. And, of course, she picked on me as being a "country girl." One day, she beat me up on the seven-block walk that I had home from school.

Even after several other attacks, I never told on her. I had an umbrella with me one day when she decided to get me again. I let her have it with the handle of the umbrella, breaking it in the process. After that, she walked to school with me regularly and was my good friend. I never told Mom and Dad. Mom and Dad had said to me, "Get into trouble at school and you'll have more trouble at home!"

And there the snippets end. Ethel Frieda Bender suffered a broken hip, which led to surgery, which led to a hospital-acquired infection, which led to her death at age 91.

As her daughter, I remember a few stories she told: quitting high school at age 16 to work and bring in money; paying rent to her parents, who kept it and returned it to her as a wedding present when she married my father, whom she had met at a candy shop in Belleville; moving to Indianapolis and opening a restaurant, the Tip Top Café; returning to Belleville; singing in a chorus; working at Scott Air Force Base; helping my grandparents, Nicholas and Magdalena, as they aged. Magdalena died following a broken hip at age 71; Nicholas, stiffened by arthritis, eventually entered a nursing home, where he died nine years later. They lived in a different world, one of conservation and living simply, one of happiness in small things — sweet juice from newly picked strawberries, laughter over a game of pinochle at the dining-room table.

The older I grow, the more I appreciate that world. There is pleasure in simplicity. There is happiness in a nature-centered life. Would I want the hardships they endured? No. Could I become totally self-reliant? Not living in a condo without a hint of a garden. But I feel privileged to have taken a small part in the lives of Nicholas and Magdelena, to have gained an appreciation for the bounteous world we live in (unless we totally screw it up). Ethel Frieda Bender bridged their world and the one of today — embracing the simple yet finding delight in the technological advances of her time. I remember the excitement when she and my dad purchased a television. Or the electric coffee pot, or the front-load washing machine.

Society moves forward, and we must move with it. But, sometimes the past should join us in that journey; this lesson from Ethel Frieda Bender and her parents enriches my life. I wish I had more of her snippets to keep reminding me that whatever it brings, life is what we make it.

Notes

www.ingramcontent.com/pod-product-compliance
Lightning Source LLC
Chambersburg PA
CBHW041401160426
42811CB00102B/1515